CHEF
ACADEMY

First American Edition 2018
Kane Miller, A Division of EDC Publishing

Copyright © 2018 Quarto Publishing plc

For information contact:
Kane Miller, A Division of EDC Publishing
PO Box 470663
Tulsa, OK 74147-0663
www.kanemiller.com
www.edcpub.com
www.usbornebooksandmore.com

Library of Congress Control Number: 2017958221

Printed in China

ISBN: 978-1-61067-715-8

1 2 3 4 5 6 7 8 9 10

CHEF
ACADEMY

WRITTEN BY
STEVE MARTIN

ILLUSTRATED BY
HANNAH BONE

Kane Miller
A DIVISION OF EDC PUBLISHING

CONTENTS

FOOD SKILLS

SOUS CHEF

HEAD CHEF

CHEF'S KIT

WELCOME TO CHEF ACADEMY!

Congratulations! You have now joined Chef Academy, where you will learn all about the different skills needed to become a chef.

Most people can prepare something to eat—even just a sandwich—but not everyone is a chef. It's not just about making delicious food, but also about managing a team of cooks in the kitchen, buying the best ingredients and making sure that your restaurant is a success.

Chefs are needed in many different places. They can be found cooking delicious meals wherever there's a kitchen—in schools, hospitals and hotels as well as in restaurants.

As you complete the tasks in this book, you will learn what a chef needs to be able to do. This includes:

- Learning about different flavors
- Exploring new cooking methods
- Creating recipes
- Planning a menu

Before you enroll at Chef Academy, read the Academy Agreement carefully and sign it.

ACADEMY AGREEMENT

Safety is the first rule of cooking. I will **never** use kitchen equipment without checking with an adult. I will **never** use a stove or oven without an adult's help.

Signed: ....

You can now fill in your Trainee Chef card.

FIRST NAME:

LAST NAME:

AGE:

DATE JOINED:

CHEF SKILLS

At Chef Academy, you will learn everything you need to become a fully qualified chef. A trainee chef has a lot to learn.

FOOD SKILLS

In this section, you will learn basic food skills, such as how to follow a recipe and how to season food. You will learn about nutrients (the essential vitamins and minerals in food that keep us healthy), find out about different types of food and discover different dishes from around the world.

SOUS CHEF

A sous chef is second in command to the head chef, and is responsible for preparing food and keeping the kitchen safe and clean. In the Sous Chef section, you will learn all about the layout of a kitchen, types of cooking equipment and different ways of cooking.

HEAD CHEF

A head chef is the most skilled person in the kitchen and manages a team of chefs. In the Head Chef section, you will learn how to plan a menu, present food, manage finances and lead your team.

NUTRITION

Think about your favorite food. How does it make you feel? For most people, eating a tasty meal is enjoyable. But food has an even more important job—it is fuel that keeps us alive. Chemicals in food called nutrients keep us strong and help our bodies grow. It's important to have a balanced diet that includes these five types of nutrients, plus fiber.

CARBOHYDRATES give us energy. Foods full of carbohydrates include bread and pasta.

MINERALS include elements such as iron, which helps our blood work properly. Iron is found in foods such as chicken and red meat.

VITAMINS keep us healthy in different ways. Vitamin C is good for skin, while vitamin A helps our eyes. Vitamins are found in lots of foods, including fresh vegetables.

FAT helps the body process vitamins and gives us long-lasting energy. Dairy products, as well as lots of other foods, contain fat.

PROTEIN helps the body repair muscles and keep them strong. Foods that contain protein include seafood and nuts.

Although it is not a nutrient, **FIBER** is important for healthy digestion because it helps us go to the bathroom. Fiber is found in foods such as fruit and beans.

PILE UP YOUR PLATE

A chef needs to serve meals that are healthy, as well as delicious. Using the information on page 10, draw a tasty meal that includes at least four different types of nutrients.

When you have drawn your meal, place your Task Complete sticker here.

PLACE STICKER HERE

TASK COMPLETE

FOOD GROUPS

A chef can use many different ingredients to make countless different meals. However, food can be separated into basic groups.

GRAINS are harvested from rice and other crops such as corn, wheat and oats. Pasta and bread are made from grains.

DAIRY products are made with milk from cows, goats or other animals. Cheese and ice cream are both dairy products.

Anything that is grown and contains seeds is a **FRUIT**. Lots of fruits, such as bananas, taste sweet, however some fruits, such as tomatoes, are savory.

VEGETABLES are grown and come in many different varieties, such as lettuce, carrots, potatoes and onions.

There are many different kinds of **SEAFOOD**, including fish such as tuna, and shellfish such as shrimp.

Beef, chicken and lamb are all types of **MEAT**.

WHAT'S IN THE SANDWICH?

A chef can create a meal with a balance of different flavors by using ingredients from different food groups. Identify each of the food groups in this sandwich. Some may be featured more than once.

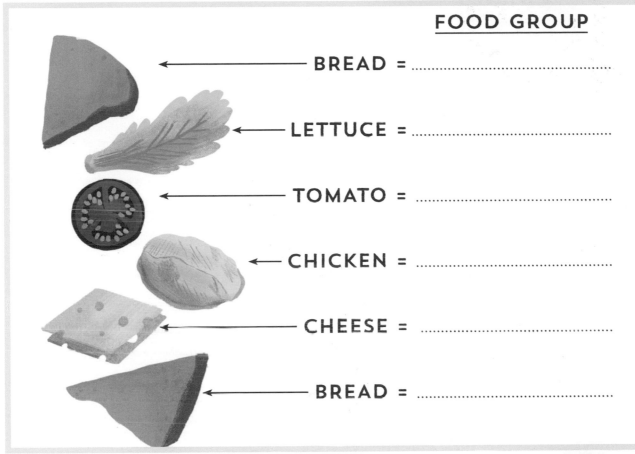

FOOD GROUP

BREAD = ...

LETTUCE = ...

TOMATO = ...

CHICKEN = ...

CHEESE = ...

BREAD = ...

When you have identified each food group, check your answers below and place your Task Complete sticker here.

PLACE STICKER HERE

ANSWERS Bread = grain. Lettuce = vegetable. Tomato = fruit. Chicken = meat. Cheese = dairy. Bread = grain.

TASK COMPLETE

IT'S ALL ABOUT
—THE TASTE—

FOOD SKILLS

Find a mirror and stick out your tongue. Can you see bumps? Your taste buds are inside these bumps, and they tell you whether the food you are eating is sweet, salty, savory, sour or bitter.

Your taste buds can identify five basic tastes. Chefs combine those five tastes in different ways to create different flavors.

Your taste buds and nose work as a team to tell you how your food tastes—you might notice that food loses its flavor when your nose is stuffy.

SWEET

SALTY

SAVORY (also known as umami)

SOUR

BITTER

TASTE TEST

A chef needs to develop a good sense of taste. You are going to carry out a test on your taste buds.

You will need: four different types of food, a bandana or eye mask, an adult helper.

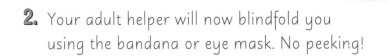

1. Ask your adult helper to prepare the four different foods while you wait in another room.

2. Your adult helper will now blindfold you using the bandana or eye mask. No peeking!

3. Your adult helper will give you each bit of food to taste, one at a time. Describe the flavor of each food out loud as you taste, and try to guess what it is.

4. Once you have finished, take off your blindfold. Did you guess correctly?

5. You can make the test more challenging by picking four similar things. For example, you could use four different types of fruit, four different drinks and so on.

When you have completed the Taste Test, place your Task Complete sticker here.

PLACE STICKER HERE

TASK COMPLETE

SEASONING

Once a chef has developed a good sense of taste, the next step is to learn how to season food. Seasoning a dish means adding something extra to the main ingredients to bring a new flavor. Not all seasonings work—you wouldn't put salt in your orange juice or sugar on your french fries!

The two best-known seasonings are **SALT AND PEPPER**. Most food tastes better with a dash of salt and pepper, so they are very important to a chef.

The leaf of a plant used to flavor food is called an **HERB**. There are many different herbs, including rosemary, mint and sage. They can be used fresh from the plant, or dried.

SPICES are the dried seeds, roots and berries of a plant. They are often ground into a powder. Examples include cinnamon and paprika.

ACIDIC flavors, such as lemon, lime and vinegar, are used to bring another layer of taste to food. For example, lemon is often served with fish, and balsamic vinegar tastes delicious with strawberries.

CHILIES, used either fresh or dried, make food taste spicy. Some people love hot food, while others can't stand the heat, so chilies need to be used carefully!

GROW YOUR OWN HERB PLANT

Pre-cut herbs can be bought at the supermarket, but freshly cut herbs taste better and are cheaper. Grow your own herb plant to use for seasoning food.

You will need: a 6-inch-deep plant pot, potting soil, a small indoor herb plant (such as parsley, rosemary, mint, basil, chives or sage), a small plate, water.

1. Fill half the plant pot with potting soil. Place the herb plant in the pot and spread out the roots. Fill the rest of the pot with potting soil, leaving about an inch of space at the top.

2. Put the plant pot on the small plate—this will catch water that drains out of the holes at the bottom of the pot. Place it near a window so it gets lots of sunlight.

3. Water the plant to help it grow, and remember that some herbs don't need a lot of water. Push your finger into the soil every so often. If it feels dry, water your plant.

4. When you need the herb for a dish, snip a few leaves from the plant. How many other herb plants can you grow?

When you have potted your herb plant, place your Task Complete sticker here.

PLACE STICKER HERE

TASK COMPLETE

17

A WORLD OF FOOD

Every country has its own kind of food. Some dishes become so popular that they spread across the globe; curry was first made in India, but is now eaten in many parts of the world. A chef can discover new ingredients by studying food from different countries.

NAME THAT FOOD

Match each dish below with its name and the country it comes from. Write the dish number in the flags on the opposite page.

DISH 1
This **GREEN** dip is often made by mashing avocados with chilies, lime juice, cilantro and garlic.

DISH 2
This dish has a **PASTRY** base. It is baked, then served with whipped cream. It is eaten during holidays, such as Thanksgiving.

DISH 3
The beets in this soup give it a **DARK-RED** color. It is often served with sour cream.

DISH 4
This food has a base of **DOUGH AND TOMATO SAUCE**. It can be topped with cheese, meat, vegetables or fish.

DISH 5
This **CRESCENT-SHAPED** breakfast food is made by rolling and folding layers of buttery pastry. It can be savory or sweet.

DISH 6
This dish is flavored with Scotch bonnet chilies, which are very spicy. It is rubbed with seasoning, then **GRILLED OR BARBECUED**.

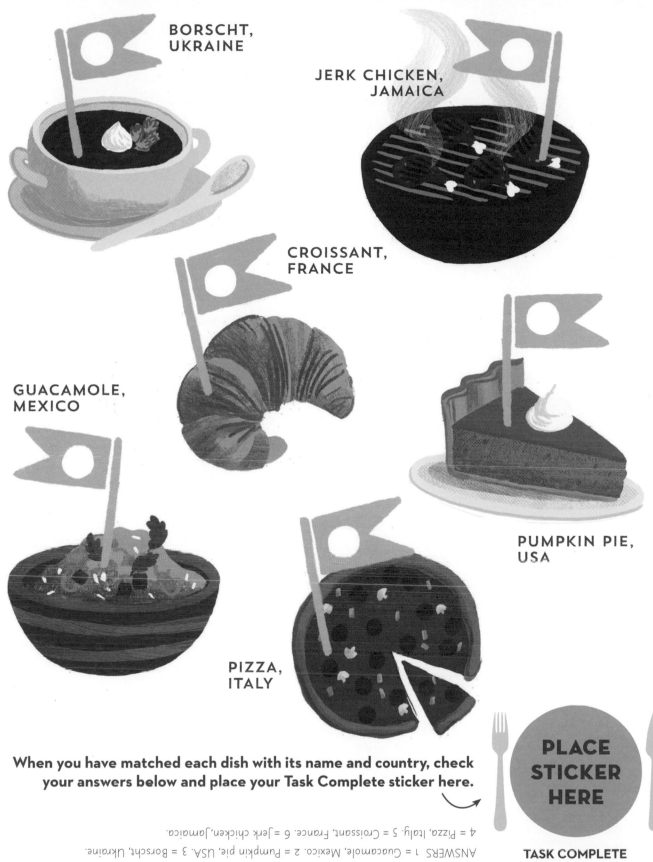

BORSCHT, UKRAINE

JERK CHICKEN, JAMAICA

CROISSANT, FRANCE

GUACAMOLE, MEXICO

PUMPKIN PIE, USA

PIZZA, ITALY

When you have matched each dish with its name and country, check your answers below and place your Task Complete sticker here.

PLACE STICKER HERE

ANSWERS 1 = Guacamole, Mexico. 2 = Pumpkin pie, USA. 3 = Borscht, Ukraine. 4 = Pizza, Italy. 5 = Croissant, France. 6 = Jerk chicken, Jamaica.

TASK COMPLETE

FOLLOWING A RECIPE

A trainee chef must learn how to follow a recipe. A recipe tells you how to make something, and there are a number of different parts to it.

This tells you how many portions of food the recipe will make.

This is how long it will take you to prepare the food.

This is how long it takes in total, including cooking or freezing time.

Read the list of ingredients before you start so you can get everything ready.

Step-by-step instructions help you to complete the recipe in the right order.

The serving suggestion recommends seasonings, toppings and side dishes that will go well with the food.

! ALLERGY
Check that the food in this recipe is safe for you to eat.

STRAWBERRY ICE CREAM

Serves: 4

Preparation time: 10 minutes

Total time needed: 6 hours

Ingredients:

15 strawberries

1 ¼ cups heavy cream

3 ½ oz. condensed milk

Method:

1. Pull the green leaves and stalks off the strawberries
2. Put the strawberries into a mixing bowl. Mash them with the back of a fork.
3. Add the heavy cream and use your fork to mix it with the strawberries.
4. Add the condensed milk and combine well.
5. Pour the mixture into a plastic container and leave in the freezer for 4 to 6 hours.

Serving suggestion:

Serve the ice cream in bowls. Add sprinkles, chocolate chips or other toppings.

WHICH DISH?

The ingredients needed for four different dishes are listed below. Can you identify which ingredient list is for which dish?

1.

INGREDIENTS:
lettuce, tomatoes, red onion, cucumber

DISH: ....

2.

INGREDIENTS:
cherries, flour, butter, egg, sugar

DISH: ....

DISHES

CHICKEN CURRY

CHERRY PIE

GREEN SALAD

SPAGHETTI AND MEATBALLS

3.

INGREDIENTS:
spaghetti, ground beef, tomato sauce, garlic, onions

DISH: ....

4.

INGREDIENTS:
chicken, peppers, cumin, tomatoes, chili, garlic

DISH: ....

When you have matched the dish to its ingredients, check your answers below and place your Task Complete sticker here.

PLACE STICKER HERE

ANSWERS 1 = Green salad. 2 = Cherry pie. 3 = Spaghetti and meatballs. 4 = Chicken curry.

TASK COMPLETE

21

—FRUITS AND—
VEGETABLES

Chefs work in places, such as schools and health-care facilities, where it is important to make healthy meals. A healthy meal includes lots of fruits and vegetables, which contain vitamins that our bodies need. Eating plenty of these foods can also help prevent illness.

There are many ways to use fruits and vegetables. A chef might serve vegetables with fish as a main course, or make a delicious dessert using fruit. Other ideas include making salads, stir-fries, vegetable soups and fruit juices.

Look at this example of a shopping list that a chef might use. Check off the fruits and vegetables that you eat regularly.

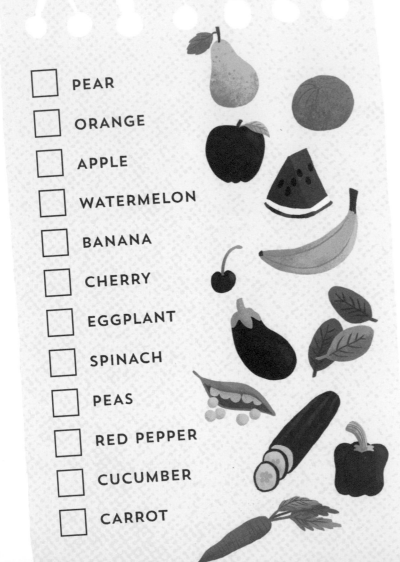

- ☐ PEAR
- ☐ ORANGE
- ☐ APPLE
- ☐ WATERMELON
- ☐ BANANA
- ☐ CHERRY
- ☐ EGGPLANT
- ☐ SPINACH
- ☐ PEAS
- ☐ RED PEPPER
- ☐ CUCUMBER
- ☐ CARROT

WHO AM I?

Can you identify the four mystery fruits and vegetables below? Read the clues and write your answers in the boxes.

1. Grow in bunches
2. Most common types are red and green
3. Used to make jam, jelly and juice

ANSWER:

1. Grows in the ground
2. Can be mashed, fried, roasted or boiled
3. Used to make chips and fries

ANSWER:

1. Grows on a plant
2. Eaten as a pizza topping, often with ham
3. Has spiky leaves

ANSWER:

1. Made up of lots of layers
2. Cooked with garlic as a base for many recipes
3. Makes people cry when it is chopped

ANSWER:

When you have identified the mystery fruits and vegetables, check your answers below and place your Task Complete sticker here.

PLACE STICKER HERE

TASK COMPLETE

ANSWERS A = Grapes. B = Potato. C = Pineapple. D = Onion.

FRUIT SALAD RECIPE

Practice following a recipe to make a delicious dessert.
Ask an adult for help. Use the tips below.

FRUIT SALAD

Serves: 2

Preparation time: 10 minutes

Total time needed: 10 minutes

Ingredients:

½ orange

½ apple

½ banana

8 strawberries

10 grapes

¼ cup fresh orange juice

TIP: To make this recipe for four people instead of two, double the amount of ingredients.

Method:

1. Peel the orange and separate the segments, then use a table knife to chop them up.
2. Chop the apple into small pieces, removing the core and any seeds.
3. Peel the banana and then slice it.
4. Pull the green leaves and stems off the strawberries and then cut them in half.
5. Cut the grapes in half lengthwise.
6. Mix all the fruit together in a bowl.
7. Pour the orange juice over the fruit.

TIP: Recipes often use teaspoons and tablespoons. Teaspoons are the little spoons; tablespoons are the bigger spoons.

!

ALLERGY

Check that the food in this recipe is safe for you to eat.

Serving suggestion:

Serve the fruit salad in bowls.

A chef can add their signature to a dish they have created by giving it a name. Think of a name for the dessert you have made and write it below.

DISH OF THE DAY

....

....

....

Remember that a recipe is just a guide. You can change a recipe as much as you like to improve it or to suit your taste. Next time, add different kinds of fruit, use lime juice or grape juice, or add cream. It's entirely up to the chef—that's you!

When you have made your fruit salad, place your Task Complete sticker here.

PLACE STICKER HERE

TASK COMPLETE

FANTASTIC FOOD!

Food is even more amazing than you might think. Check out these fascinating food facts.

Thirsty? You could try a cup of the world's most expensive **COFFEE**, although you might want to know first that it is made from poop! An animal called a civet eats coffee beans. After the beans have passed through the animal, they are taken from its poop, washed and ground up to make coffee.

Feeling hungry? The world's largest dish is a **MIDDLE EASTERN** specialty. Eggs are stuffed inside fish. The fish are then put inside chickens, and the chickens are stuffed inside a cooked sheep. Finally, the sheep is placed inside a whole roast camel!

Most **CARROTS** eaten today are orange, but did you know that purple carrots were once more common?

Ripe **CRANBERRIES** can bounce like a rubber ball

CHEF INFO

A single **COW** produces enough meat to make 700-800 burgers!

26

FOOD SKILLS

NAME:

- -

The above-named chef has now completed
the **FOOD SKILLS** course.

Chef Academy would like to
thank you for your hard work.

WELL DONE!

QUALIFICATION DATE:

- - - - - - - - - - - - - - - - - - - -

SOUS CHEF

THE KITCHEN

OVEN AND STOVE

SERVING COUNTER

VEGETABLE PREPARATION AREA

As a sous chef, it's important to understand how a kitchen is organized. Use the stickers at the back of the book to complete the picture.

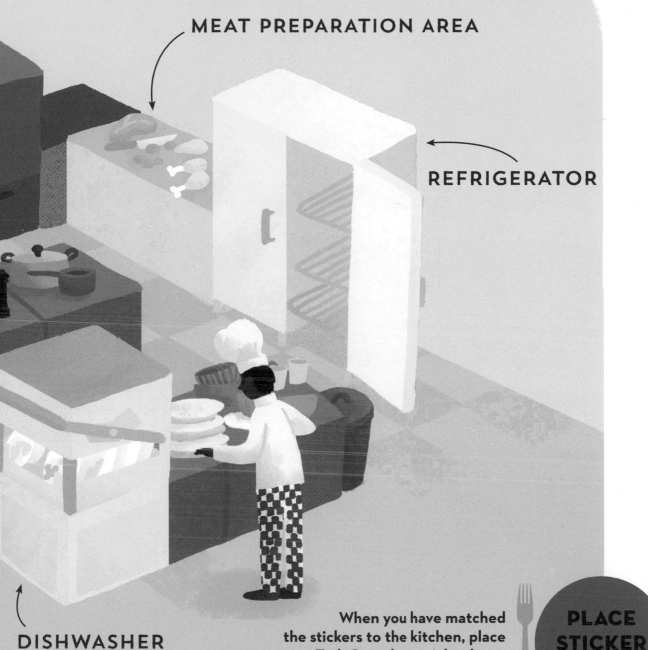

MEAT PREPARATION AREA

REFRIGERATOR

DISHWASHER

When you have matched the stickers to the kitchen, place your Task Complete sticker here.

PLACE STICKER HERE

TASK COMPLETE

-KITCHEN- EQUIPMENT

SOUS CHEF

When you go into a kitchen, you will see lots of different tools. Here are some of the most common.

GRATER: for grating cheese and other food

WHISK: for mixing food

SPATULA: for mixing, spreading and lifting food

OVEN MITT: for protecting hands from heat

LADLE: for scooping soups and liquids

KNIFE: for cutting food

PANS: for cooking on a stove

ROLLING PIN: for rolling dough

WHISKING CHALLENGE

**Different kitchen equipment is used for different tasks.
The most common use for a whisk is to mix ingredients together.**

You will need: a large mixing bowl, a teaspoon of dishwashing liquid, a cup of water, a whisk.

1. Pour the water into the mixing bowl and add the dishwashing liquid.

2. Hold the bowl firmly with one hand, and the whisk with the other. Mix the dishwashing liquid into the water by moving the whisk from side to side as quickly as you can.

3. As you whisk, you should see lots of bubbles. This is because the water and the dishwashing liquid have mixed together.

When you have completed the Whisking Challenge, place your Task Complete sticker here.

PLACE STICKER HERE

TASK COMPLETE

THE MANY WAYS —TO COOK—

Food is cooked by heating it up. There are lots of different ways to cook food. Read about some of them below.

When food is **BROILED**, it is placed underneath a heat source.

FRYING is a good way to cook small amounts of food quickly. The food is placed in a large shallow pan with hot oil or fat.

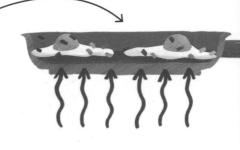

When food is **BOILED**, it is cooked in a pan of very hot water.

BARBECUING is grilling done outdoors over a gas or charcoal barbecue. Smoke from charcoal flavors the food.

Meat and vegetables are **ROASTED** in the oven, while bread and cakes are **BAKED**. An oven is good for cooking large pieces of food over a long period of time.

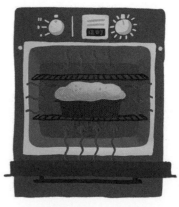

SOUS CHEF

WHAT'S COOKING?

Draw something frying and boiling on the stove, and something roasting or baking in the oven.

When you have completed the picture, place your Task Complete sticker here.

PLACE STICKER HERE

TASK COMPLETE

33

—FOOD— HYGIENE

When working with food, it is important to keep the kitchen and yourself clean. If you don't, your customers could become very sick. This is called food hygiene and it is so important that, in many countries, kitchens are inspected to make sure they are clean, and chefs have to pass food-hygiene exams.

Some of the most important food-hygiene rules are listed here.

* Wash your hands.
* Wear clean clothes and aprons.
* Tie back long hair.
* Do not prepare or cook food if you are sick.
* Use different knives and chopping boards for raw meat and ready-to-eat food.
* Make sure meat is cooked correctly.
* Do not use food that is past its expiration date.
* Keep a lid on trash cans.
* No animals in the kitchen.
* Keep food preparation areas and floors clean.

KITCHEN INSPECTION

Carry out an inspection on this kitchen by drawing a circle around the food-hygiene problems you can see. Can you find all eight?

When you have completed the Kitchen Inspection, check your answers below and place your Task Complete sticker here.

ANSWERS 1. Trash can without lid. 2. Rat in the kitchen. 3. A sick chef. 4. The chefs have dirty aprons. 5. Food that is past its expiration date. 6. Spill on the floor. 7. Dirty food preparation areas. 8. A chef with long hair that is not tied back.

TASK COMPLETE

PLACE STICKER HERE

PREPARING FOOD

Although some foods, such as rice, fruit and salad, should be prepared right before serving, other foods can be prepared in advance. Preparing food and ingredients in advance saves time and means that a meal will reach the table more quickly.

Soup can be made before the restaurant opens.

If bread or cake is on the menu, it needs to be baked before service begins.

Chicken takes a few hours to roast, so it needs to be cooked in advance.

Vegetables can be peeled and sliced hours before they're needed.

PREP TIME

Look at today's menu. Can you identify which foods to prepare in advance, and which to prepare right before serving? Write your answers on the prep list below.

MENU OF THE DAY

APPETIZER
TOMATO SOUP WITH HOMEMADE BREAD

ENTRÉE
ROAST CHICKEN, RICE AND SALAD

DESSERT
CHOCOLATE CAKE WITH FRESH STRAWBERRIES

PREPARE IN ADVANCE

....
....
....
....

PREPARE JUST BEFORE SERVING

....
....
....

When you have completed the prep list, check your answers below and place your Task Complete sticker here.

PLACE STICKER HERE

TASK COMPLETE

ANSWERS Foods to prepare in advance = tomato soup, homemade bread, roast chicken, chocolate cake. Foods to prepare right before serving = rice, salad, fresh strawberries.

—FOOD— STORAGE

A sous chef needs to keep the kitchen organized and safe. It is important to know how to store food properly so that it stays fresh and is good to eat.

Milk, yogurt and cooked meats need to be kept cold in a **REFRIGERATOR** to prevent them from spoiling.

Raw meat, chicken and fish must always be kept on the **BOTTOM SHELF**. This stops bacteria from spreading to other food.

A **FREEZER** must have a temperature of 0°F or below.

Freezing food means it can be kept for **A LONG TIME** without going bad.

Foods with a long life, such as pasta, sugar and rice, can be kept at room temperature in **DRY STORAGE**.

Food in dry storage must be kept in packages or containers. This is to prevent attracting **PESTS**, such as rats or cockroaches.

FOOD DETECTIVE

See what you can find in the storage spaces in your home. Record your findings below.

In the refrigerator:

....

....

....

....

In the freezer:

....

....

....

....

In dry storage:

....

....

....

....

When you have recorded your findings, place your Task Complete sticker here.

PLACE STICKER HERE

TASK COMPLETE

ORDERS

A menu is designed to give customers lots of different choices. A large menu can mean that the kitchen needs to cook many different meals all at once.

A table of customers must be served their food together, so that everyone can eat at the same time. However, some meals take longer to cook than others. A sous chef needs excellent time-management skills to decide what should be cooked first.

ORDER UP!

The six meals below must all be served at 8 p.m. For each dish, look at how long it takes to cook, then figure out what time it needs to start cooking. Use the clock to help you.

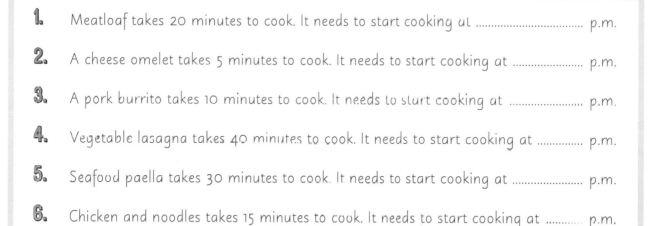

1. Meatloaf takes 20 minutes to cook. It needs to start cooking at .... p.m.

2. A cheese omelet takes 5 minutes to cook. It needs to start cooking at .... p.m.

3. A pork burrito takes 10 minutes to cook. It needs to start cooking at .... p.m.

4. Vegetable lasagna takes 40 minutes to cook. It needs to start cooking at .... p.m.

5. Seafood paella takes 30 minutes to cook. It needs to start cooking at .... p.m.

6. Chicken and noodles takes 15 minutes to cook. It needs to start cooking at .... p.m.

When you have written the cooking times, check your answers below and place your Task Complete sticker here.

PLACE STICKER HERE

TASK COMPLETE

ANSWERS 1 = 7:40 p.m. 2 = 7:55 p.m. 3 = 7:50 p.m. 4 = 7:20 p.m. 5 = 7:30 p.m. 6 = 7:45 p.m.

MEASURING

Measuring ingredients is an essential part of cooking. Find out about different kinds of measurements and measuring tools below.

PINCH, **SPLASH** and **DROP** all mean a very small amount.

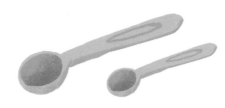

Spoons are often used to measure out ingredients. A **TABLESPOON** (tbs.) holds three times more than a **TEASPOON** (tsp.).

A **SCALE** shows ounces (oz.) and pounds (lb.).

A **MEASURING CUP** usually shows cup measurements, as well as fluid ounces (fl. oz.).

MEASURING CHALLENGE

Practice your measuring skills by completing the challenges below.

You will need: a scale, pasta or rice, a measuring cup, a set of measuring spoons.

CHALLENGE 1
Which do you think is heavier: 1 lb. flour or 1 lb. pasta? Write your answer below.

CHALLENGE 2
How many ¼ teaspoon measures are in 1 teaspoon measure? Write your answer below.

CHALLENGE 3
Using the scale, measure 8 oz. pasta or rice. Check the box once you have completed this challenge.

CHALLENGE 4
Using a measuring cup, measure 8 fl. oz. water. Check the box once you have completed this challenge.

CHALLENGE 5
Using a set of spoons, measure the following amounts of water: ¼ teaspoon, ½ teaspoon, 1 tablespoon. Check the box once you have completed this challenge.

When you have completed the Measuring Challenge, check your answers below and place your Task Complete sticker here.

PLACE STICKER HERE

TASK COMPLETE

ANSWERS: Challenge 1 = 1 lb. flour and 1 lb. pasta weigh the same. Challenge 2 = Four ¼ teaspoon measures are in 1 teaspoon measure.

WHO'S WHO IN THE
RESTAURANT

A restaurant is a very busy place, and it's important to get to know your team. To understand how the kitchen works, you need to be familiar with these three key roles.

A **DISHWASHER** makes sure that there are clean plates, cutlery and kitchen utensils. They keep the kitchen clean, unload deliveries, and may also chop vegetables and help as needed.

A **WAITER** takes care of the customers, takes orders and serves food. They may also help the customers by recommending dishes. Waiters are the essential link between the kitchen and the customers.

Every restaurant needs a **MANAGER**. This is the person who hires staff, leads the team of waiters, and carries out lots of other management tasks.

CHEF INFO

SOUS CHEF

NAME:

The above-named chef has now completed the
SOUS CHEF course.

Chef Academy would like to
thank you for your hard work.

WELL DONE!

QUALIFICATION DATE:

LOOKING THE PART

A chef looks very professional in their uniform, but their clothes are not just for show.

The **HAT** keeps hair away from food. A chef with long hair might wear a hairnet.

The thick **APRON** protects against spills. It is made from flame-resistant material.

The **JACKET** is made of strong fabric that protects against spills and burns, and keeps the chef cool in the hot kitchen.

The **PANTS** are dark or patterned to hide stains. They are loose for comfort, and to keep spilled food and liquid away from the chefs skin.

The **SHOES** are comfortable, because a chef spends lots of time standing up. They are sturdy and will protect the chefs feet if anything is dropped.

MAKE A CHEF'S HAT

You will need: a long piece of white craft paper about 3 inches wide, scissors, white crepe paper, tape, an adult helper.

1. Ask an adult to wrap the long piece of craft paper to fit around your head, leaving some overlap. Use the scissors to cut away any excess paper.

2. Lay the long piece of craft paper on a flat surface. Unfold the crepe paper and tape it lengthwise to the craft paper.

3. Once all of the crepe paper is stuck down, tape the two ends of the craft paper together, making sure that they overlap. Then, tape the crepe paper together at the top on the inside.

4. Fold the top of the hat inward so that the crepe paper puffs out. Your hat is now ready to wear!

When you have made your chef's hat, place your Task Complete sticker here.

PLACE STICKER HERE

TASK COMPLETE

47

A THREE-COURSE —MEAL—

There are lots of different ways to organize meals, but the most popular is the three-course meal. This involves serving the customer three different dishes.

The **APPETIZER** is a small amount of food served at the beginning of a meal. Having an appetizer gives the customer variety, and something small to eat while the chef is preparing the entrée.

The **ENTRÉE** is the largest dish. It could be anything from noodles to steamed fish with vegetables.

Finally, **DESSERT** is served. This is a sweet-tasting dish; examples include cake, ice cream, fruit pie or pastry.

THREE-COURSE CHOICE

Sanjay is hungry! Read his preferences below, then draw a three-course meal catered to his taste. Remember to have variety between the courses.

* He prefers hot food to cold food.
* He often chooses chicken dishes.
* He doesn't enjoy spicy food.
* His favorite fruit is peaches.

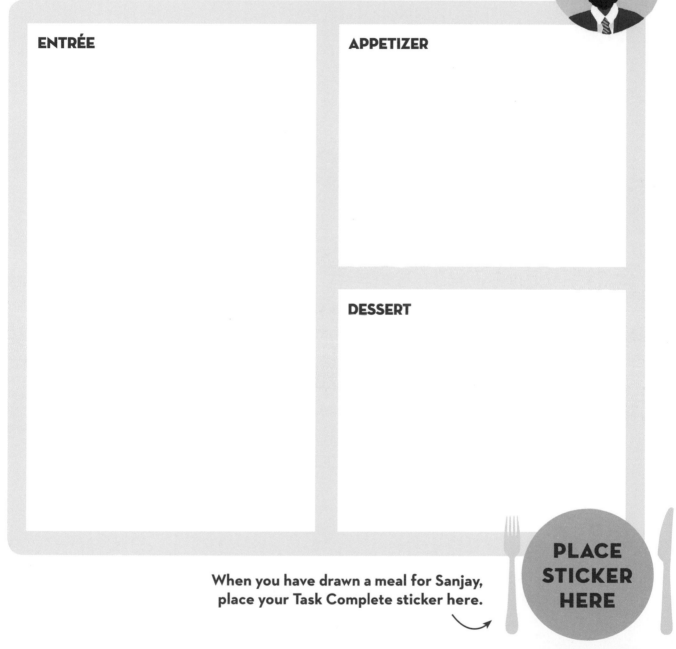

ENTRÉE

APPETIZER

DESSERT

When you have drawn a meal for Sanjay, place your Task Complete sticker here.

PLACE STICKER HERE

TASK COMPLETE

49

—MENU— PLANNING

An important part of a head chef's job is planning the menu. A restaurant can't supply every type of food, but at the same time, a restaurant has to offer a good choice of meals.

Two appetizers, two entrées and two desserts gives a choice of eight different three-course meals.

Appetizer A

Entrée A   **Entrée B**

Dessert A   **Dessert B**   **Dessert A**   **Dessert B**

Appetizer B

Entrée A   **Entrée B**

Dessert A   **Dessert B**   **Dessert A**   **Dessert B**

10 appetizers, 100 entrées and 10 desserts would give a choice of 1,000 different three-course meals!

PLAN A MENU

You are going to plan a menu. You need four appetizers, six entrées and four desserts (this gives nearly 100 different combinations). Try to have variety. For example, if you choose soup as one appetizer, make sure the other three appetizers are different.

APPETIZERS

....
....
....
....

ENTRÉES

....
....
....
....
....
....

Think about food you like or meals you have seen in restaurants.

DESSERTS

....
....
....
....

When you have completed your menu, place your Task Complete sticker here.

PLACE STICKER HERE

TASK COMPLETE

—LEADING— YOUR TEAM

TABLE 5 WANTS THEIR FOOD NOW!

GET THE CHICKEN OUT OF THE OVEN!

As a head chef, it's your job to lead your staff and make sure they work together as a team. Besides creating delicious food, a head chef needs to:

* Make sure all ingredients needed are available.
* Plan the team so there are enough chefs and dishwashers to work.
* Decide how the team works—one chef might focus on appetizers, while another one cooks entrées and a third makes desserts.
* Face any problems that arise, from faulty equipment to staff shortages.
* Supervise the team and make sure they all know what they need to do.

THE GRILL'S NOT WORKING!

You need to make sure the staff are happy and want to do the best job they can. A successful head chef has a great team behind them!

WE NEED MORE CLEAN PLATES!

LEADER RECIPE

On the right are skills and attitudes that a head chef needs to lead their team. Choose four from each list that you think are the most important. Put your answers into the leader recipe below.

SKILLS

Communicating
Planning
Problem solving
Time management
Teaching
Decision making
Organizing
Motivating people

ATTITUDES

Good attention to detail
Positive
Calm
Perfectionist
Passionate
Helpful
Friendly
Sense of humor

LEADER RECIPE

1 package ....

5 oz. ....

½ cup ....

3 fl. oz. ....

1 tbs. ....

1 tsp. ....

A splash of ....

A pinch of ....

Mix well to create the perfect leader!

When you have created your Leader Recipe, place your Task Complete sticker here.

PLACE STICKER HERE

TASK COMPLETE

HOW MUCH?

When planning a menu, a head chef needs to think about more than what to cook. A restaurant needs to make money to pay for the ingredients, kitchen equipment, staff, rent and other bills.

A good way of approaching this is to charge the customer three times what the food costs to buy. See the example below.

A restaurant has a hamburger with fries on the menu.

Hamburger costs **$1.00**

Burger bun costs **$0.40**

Lettuce costs **$0.20**

Tomato costs **$0.30**

Red onion costs **$0.10**

Fries cost **$0.50**

TOTAL: $2.50

The customer pays three times the amount that the hamburger and fries cost the restaurant to buy.

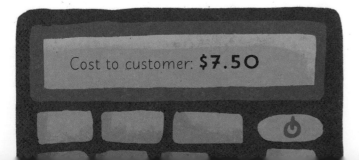

Cost to customer: **$7.50**

MENU MATH

Using the costs shown here, add the missing food prices to the menu below. Remember that you need to charge three times the cost of the food.

SALMON FILLET **$3.00**

BROCCOLI **$0.50**

BAGEL **$0.50**

LENTIL CURRY **$1.00**

RICE **$0.50**

PEANUT BUTTER **$0.30**

MENU

MEAL A Salmon fillet + broccoli = $ _ _ . _ _

MEAL B Lentil curry + rice = $ _ . _ _

MEAL C Bagel + peanut butter = $ _ . _ _

When you have priced the menu, check your answers below and place your Task Complete sticker here.

PLACE STICKER HERE

TASK COMPLETE

A FEAST FOR THE EYES

Feel like eating a bowl of splodge? Why not? It might taste delicious …

The problem with a bowl of splodge is that whatever it might taste like, it looks horrible! A head chef needs to make sure that each dish that leaves their kitchen appeals to the eyes as much as the mouth. Good presentation means thinking about colors, shapes and patterns.

A chef can be really creative with ideas. For example, a basic chocolate cake can be decorated so that it looks very special.

STRAWBERRY MOUSE

Even something as simple as a strawberry can be transformed into a snack that looks amazing. Try the recipe below to practice your presentation skills.

You will need: a strawberry, small tube of black icing, mini chocolate chips, sliced almonds, red licorice laces, an adult helper.

1. Pull the green leaves and stem off a strawberry. Ask your adult helper to slice the strawberry lengthwise so that it sits flat.

2. Use a dot of black icing to attach the mini chocolate chips to the strawberry as eyes and a nose.

3. Ask your adult helper to cut two slits in the top of the strawberry. Place a sliced almond into each slit for ears.

4. Push the end of a length of licorice lace into the back end of the strawberry for the tail.

When you have made your Strawberry Mouse, place your Task Complete sticker here.

PLACE STICKER HERE

TASK COMPLETE

VEGETABLE STIR-FRY
—RECIPE—

Making a vegetable stir-fry is all about the preparation. You will need to ask an adult helper to cook the stir-fry, as it involves working with heat. It's best to make a stir-fry in a wok, because it will keep the vegetables crisp, but use a large frying pan if you don't have a wok.

VEGETABLE STIR-FRY

Serves: 4

Preparation time: 10 minutes

Total time needed: 30 minutes

Ingredients:

1 carrot

6 button mushrooms

1 green pepper

1 red onion

8 oz. dried egg noodles

2 tbs. vegetable oil

2 tbs. soy sauce

A handful of cilantro leaves

⚠ ALLERGY
Check that the food in this recipe is safe for you to eat.

1. Ask your adult helper to peel the carrot, then grate it.

2. Clean the mushrooms with a damp piece of paper towel, then, using a table knife, cut them into small pieces.

3. Using a table knife, cut the green pepper in half. Pull out the stalk and seeds and, with a table knife, cut away the white parts. Slice the pepper into strips.

4. Ask your adult helper to peel and chop the red onion into small pieces.

5. Ask your adult helper to cook the noodles in boiling water for 4 minutes, then drain them.

6. Ask your adult helper to heat the oil in a wok or large frying pan over a high heat, then add the vegetables.

7. Cook the vegetables for 3 minutes, stirring the vegetables all the time with a spatula—you can do this as long as your adult helper supervises.

8. Add the noodles and soy sauce, then cook for another 2 minutes, stirring often —you can do this as long as your adult helper supervises.

9. Turn off the heat and serve.

Serving suggestion:
Serve in bowls, topped with chopped cilantro.

When you have made and tasted your stir-fry, place your Task Complete sticker here.

PLACE STICKER HERE

TASK COMPLETE

CHASING THE STARS

Undercover inspectors visit restaurants to try the food and decide how good it is. There are many different systems, but the best known is probably the Michelin star system, which is used around the world. Restaurants are awarded one, two or three stars.

VERY GOOD COOKING

EXCELLENT COOKING

SUPERB COOKING

An inspector has to think about things such as:

QUALITY Are the ingredients of a high standard?

COOKING Is the food well cooked? Is it burned? Is it cold?

FLAVOR Is it tasty? Do the different items go well together?

APPEARANCE Does the meal look attractive?

ORIGINALITY Is it different from what they have eaten before?

If a chef knew that an inspector was visiting, they would do everything they could to make the meal amazing. This is why inspectors go "undercover"— they need to see what the restaurant is like for a customer on a typical day.

* An inspector's job is a close-guarded secret from everyone, aside from family and friends.

* They will reserve a restaurant table using a false name.

* Before awarding any stars, an inspector might visit a restaurant several times, ordering a different meal each time.

* Inspectors will alter their appearance to avoid being recognized. They may change their hair, grow a beard, or wear glasses or a hat.

Why not keep a notebook and award stars to the meals you eat at school, home or in restaurants?

CHEF INFO

HEAD CHEF

NAME:

- -

The above-named chef has now completed
the HEAD CHEF course.

Chef Academy would like to
thank you for your hard work.

WELL DONE!

QUALIFICATION DATE:

- - - - - - - - - - - - - - - - - - - -

WELL DONE!

You have successfully completed all your tasks
and finished your trainee chefs course.

You are now ready to graduate from Chef Academy.

**AS PART OF YOUR GRADUATION CEREMONY, YOU SHOULD READ
THE CHEF'S CODE BELOW AND PROMISE TO FOLLOW IT.**

1. I will make sure that the kitchen is a clean and safe environment.
   I will follow food-hygiene rules at all times.

2. I will be extremely careful when cooking and using kitchen
   equipment, and will ask for help when I need to.

3. I will teach my staff about healthy eating. I will use lots of
   different fruits and vegetables in my cooking.

4. I will always work hard to cook the tastiest meals possible
   for my customers.

5. I will continue to learn, experiment and try new foods.

6. I will treat customers and fellow kitchen staff
   with respect at all times.

Draw or glue
a picture of
your face here.

SIGNED:

- - - - - - - - - - - - - - - - - - - -

CHEF'S KIT

- Four press-out cupcake decoration templates (on the flaps of the book)
- Stickers
- Equipment Pairs game cards
- Foods of the World poster
- Pizza Toppings game

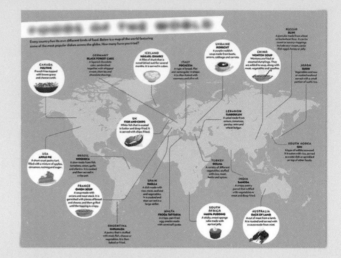

EQUIPMENT PAIRS GAME

1. Shuffle the cards, then place them in a row, facedown on a flat surface.
2. Take turns to flip over two cards of your choice. If they are a matching pair, keep them and take another turn. If not, turn the cards over and let the next player take their turn.
3. The player to collect the most pairs is the winner.

PIZZA-TOPPING GAME COUNTERS

TOPPING PIECES

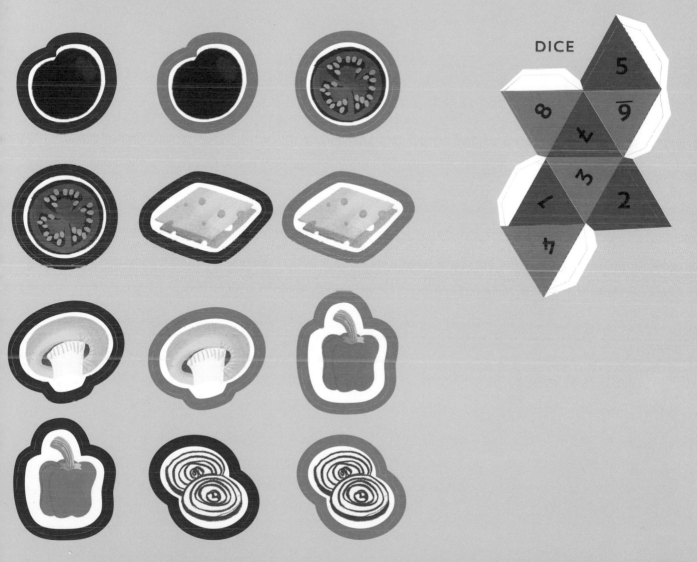

DICE

5

8   9

7

3   2

7

4

EQUIPMENT PAIRS GAME

ROLLING PIN	ROLLING PIN	WHISK	WHISK

GRATER	GRATER	LADLE	LADLE

PAN	PAN	SPATULA	SPATULA

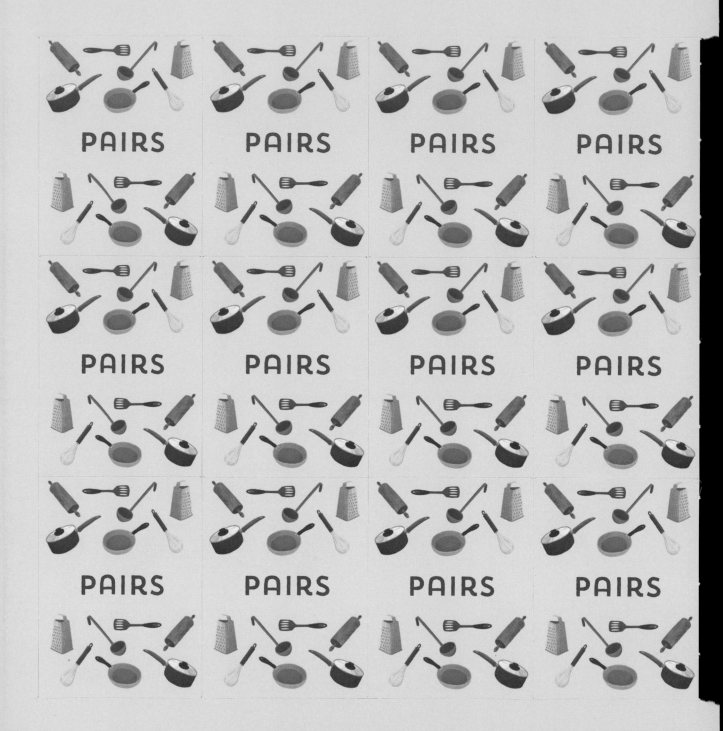